Stephen McClarence's

SHEFFIELD WALKABOUT

Illustrated by
Norah Rogerson

SHEFFIELD CITY LIBRARIES

First published 1988.

Published by Sheffield City Libraries,
Central Library, Surrey Street,
Sheffield S1 1XZ.

ISBN 086321 085 6

Printed in Great Britain by
Sheffield Printing Services.

Contents

Introduction

My grandmother worked as a domestic help. Every day, she walked from her home in Attercliffe to her employer's home in Ecclesall – and back again. My aunt worked for a while in an East End factory, and walked there and back from her Heeley home. They probably passed each other in the street from time to time.

Such walking, through towns, is now largely unnecessary. People no longer walk if they can avoid it. Sheffield people still walk in the country, of course – either fanatically walking, Clarion Rambling, heads sternly down, Ordnance Survey maps in little plastic envelopes, or, increasingly, walking round from the car's driving seat to the boot to unlock the picnic chairs which will provide easy, fume-choked seating in whichever Derbyshire layby has been chosen for this particular Golden Frame Sunday.

But, as for walking in towns . . . Our ever-increasing reliance on the motorcar – I once shared a flat with a man who took his car to the corner shop a hundred yards down the road – and the planners' kowtowing to the needs of the motorist have made life difficult for the pedestrian. At least Sheffield's planners are seeing the light. In 1987, they announced that future planning decisions would take pedestrians much more into account.

The walks in this book are designed with the urban stroller, a perhaps endangered species, in mind. They are not strenuous hikes up and down the Seven Hills of Sheffield. They are rambles round some of the city's more pleasant and characterful areas. There is, of course, a difference between "pleasant" and "characterful".

Broomhill is immeasurably pleasant, with its stone buildings and its shops selling tinned Royal Game Soup, and its atmosphere of being a place where every problem can be solved by civilised argument. Attercliffe, on the other hand, and the other side of town, is more characterful than pleasant. More than most areas in Sheffield, its present is bound up in its past and the shops that remain are full of rehoused East Enders drawn back to their roots. But its atmosphere is unfailingly powerful.

Most of the areas covered by the walks fall somewhere between these two extremes. Almost all are easily taken for granted, but endless fascination lurks on even the most apparently unexciting walk. When an acquaintance said he had seen me prowling the Queens Road area, I explained I had been plotting a walk. "Who's going to walk **there**?" he sniffed. I knew then I was on the right track, with walks that concentrate not so much on the unusual as on the absolutely typical; the ordinary rather than the extraordinary.

They explore the Sheffield of today. They aim to capture some of the flavour of different districts and are not written as scholarly essays in Early English and Perpendicular. Buildings and history obviously play their part, though churches may be only as important as pubs and banks, the twin roads to ruin and respectability. The featured buildings may be interesting more as strands in the fabric of everyday Sheffield life, for their human interest, than for their architectural distinction.

And anyway, it is dangerous to pinpoint too many buildings. What is here today may be down tomorrow. In

Introduction

November 1986, I devised a prototype Attercliffe trail for my Sheffielder column in The Star. I pointed out a couple of dozen factories, churches, chapels, shops and pubs. When I returned in November 1987 for the Attercliffe walk in this book, three of the buildings had been demolished and a fourth had been horribly modernised.

In retrospect, Norah Rogerson and I may have got in just in time. Here and there, this portrait of Sheffield today has suddenly and sometimes unexpectedly become a portrait of Sheffield yesterday—a snapshot of a fast-disappearing city. As Sheffield adapts to its new role as a post-industrial city, service industries and tourism will perhaps give people a reason for living here again. Inevitably, many buildings—including some mentioned in the walks—will be bulldozed to make way for shopping centres and leisure complexes of greater or lesser architectural distinction. Parkwood Springs (see Walk G), for instance, is becoming a ski centre, the redevelopment of the Canal Basin (see Walk F) has been given a definite go-ahead, the area around Carver Lane (see Walk E) is being partly transformed into a shopping arcade. With political pragmatism now lurking round every dinky new brick-built corner, facets of the old city's character are undoubtedly being lost. This book is to some extent an elegy for that lost Sheffield.

The walks cross the city in sometimes unexpected ways, and are arranged so they can be linked together. Sheffield's communications are defined very much by its bus routes, which radiate from the centre and make adjacent districts seem very remote from each other. Walkley and Crookes are just a steep hillside walk apart, but the No 52 goes one way and the No 95 goes another and never the twain meet. Many of the walks link these spokes, taking in some of the grand views which Sheffield, uniquely among big English cities, offers from almost every vantage point.

The approach is descriptive, historical, architectural and anecdotal by turns, and occasionally draws on research originally carried out for the Sheffielder column. The book is written as much for armchair walkers in slippers as for ramblers in sturdy boots, and the legwork of devising it has opened up all sorts of unexpected alleys and gennels to me. The walks, it's worth stressing before we start, are designed for the non-driver. They begin and end on bus routes – only one ends where it began.

Finally, in grateful acknowledgement, Peter Harvey of The Star, Martin Olive of Sheffield Local Studies Library and Mike Higginbottom have got me out of some tight historical corners, and Clare Jenkins has pointed out much that I would otherwise have missed.

Walk A:

ST LUKES CHURCH
NORTHFIELD AV.
1
2
BOLE HILL
RD.
NORTHFIELD
ROAD
DUNCAN ROAD
COOMBE
ROAD
3
CROOKES
BLAKENEY ROAD
4
LYDGATE LANE
CROOKES ROAD
HALLAMGATE RD
TAPTONVILLE
RD.
5
FULWOOD RD.
MANCHESTER
RD.
ASHGATE RD.
6
ASHDELL RD.
7
ENDCLIFFE
CRESCENT
ENDCLIFFE VALE ROAD
RIVERDALE RD
9
10
8
RUSTLINGS RD
ECCLESALL ROAD

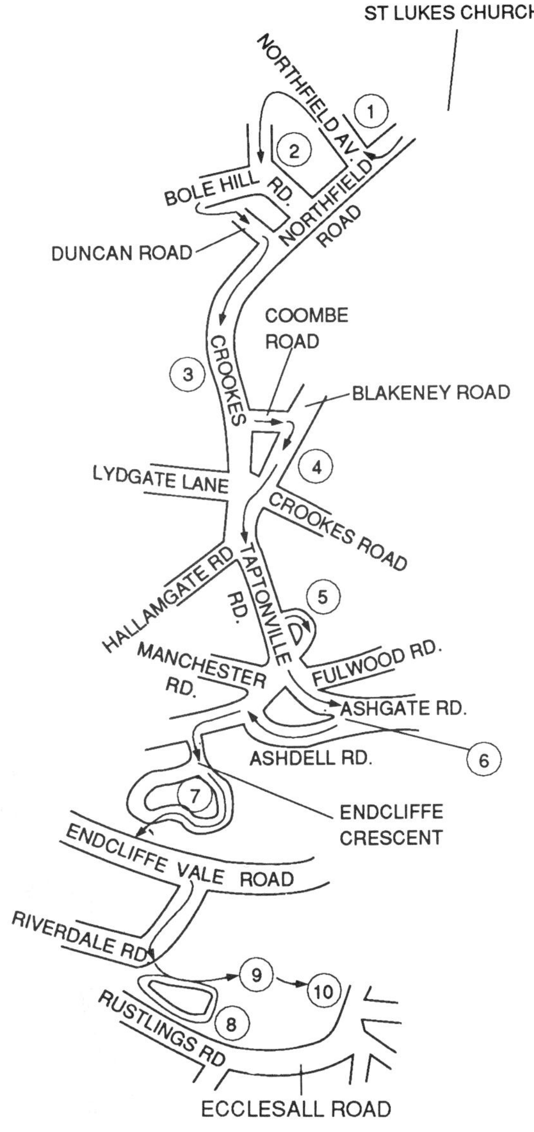

Artist's Introduction and Acknowledgments

In July 1985 I left Sheffield to live twelve miles away. Travelling back to Sheffield each day made me notice for the first time the extent of continuing redevelopment in the City. I would begin to enjoy a landscape newly created by the demolition men, only to find that view itself disappearing a few weeks later. New spaciousness enhanced remaining buildings, and created fresh vistas—or desolation, depending how you looked at it.

In 1986 I started a programme of drawing in the Bramall Lane area, but I soon realised that only a team of people could record all the constant changes—and that I needed to concentrate on a specific project.

David Hey, Reader in Local History, Division of Continuing Education, Sheffield University, and Peter Harvey of The Star helped to put me in touch with Stephen McClarence. Stephen's enthusiasm for Sheffield matched my own and he has been an inspired driving force in the creation of this book. I would like to thank the above-mentioned, plus Pat Coleman, City Librarian, who responded so promptly and supportively to the idea for this project, and City Libraries graphic designer Jill Leeming for the book design, maps and page layouts.

In my illustrations I have tried to highlight details rather than landscapes, and intentionally illustrated some buildings and details not described in the text—so I hope the text and illustrations are complementary.

Whilst I was drawing outside, the public consistently demonstrated a lively interest in the project. Some expressed strong feelings about the destruction of relatively sound and familiar property. Many drawings demanded that I return to the same site frequently, so I was able to get acquainted with people living and working in the district. To my great satisfaction, they seemed genuinely pleased that their district was being recognised and recorded.

I would particularly like to thank the following: Ms. Doreen Field of Rutland Cutlery Works, who offered to make me a brown paper apron and fetched me sandwiches from the corner shop; Changers Hair Studio of Glossop Road, the Family Planning Association and Mr. Kite's Bistro, who also allowed me to draw from the interiors of their premises; Rev. A. V. Langwith of St. Matthew's Church, Carver Street (copper panel, choir stalls); and Sue Callaghan who photocopied so willingly and cheerfully. Also those who brought out cups of tea on Meadow Terrace and Hanover Street, thus greatly relieving me from the numbing cold. Lastly, the owner of Food for Thought on Crookes, who allowed me to use the phone (three times) to sort out a minor emergency.

The English winter is not conducive to outdoor drawing, but it is excellent for walking. Perhaps this book will make a city walkabout even more stimulating; I hope so.

Norah K. Rogerson
March 1988

Crookes to Hunter's Bar

Approximate distance: 2 miles
Start: No 52 bus from city centre

The bus to Crookes climbs up and up – and just before it starts its careful descent from the top of Northfield Road, get off and turn left down Northfield Avenue (1). Even if the wind is blowing, which it probably will be, go through the gates at the end and out onto the grand and bracing heights of the Bole Hills. Here is Sheffield's Kinder, a place to get your dog blown away and once a centre for iron smelting. Long before the Romans, the more enterprising industrialists of Crookes were exploiting the gales, which rushed through the hills' rock

cavities creating wind tunnels as flame-fanningly fierce as blacksmiths' bellows. Now the Bole Hills offer an edge-of-the-world view over Rivelin and Stannington. Only up here do you realise how much Rivelin is an insolent tongue of green sticking out of the red mouth of suburbia. Turn left at the hedge before the children's playground and, with the bowling green to the right, hurtle through the high-hedged tunnel, turn right at the end and then left

and take the upper path past a sort of miniature Burbage Rocks (the directions simplify as we go on). On the left, the stone-built Cocked Hat Cottage (2) leaps out of the hill (it is actually a group of cottages, but we are too high up here to quibble over numerical niceties). The cottage commands a dazzling view, over the allotments, of rectangular fields and rectangular houses. As the path joins Bole Hill Lane, cross and continue forward and take the flight of steps on the left before the modern flats. It leads into Duncan Road and, turning left, an unexpected outcrop of suburbia, complete with monkey puzzle trees and, in the front doors, as much stained glass as Sheffield Cathedral can boast (a wise owl gazes out of No 108).

Turn right onto Crookes (the road rather than the district), from where our walk is mostly downhill, and on the corner with Marston Road admire the decorative Thirties shop frontage whose trim urns and crisp, clean lines show aspirations to somewhere far grander than Crookes. This is not to condescend. Crookes (the district rather than the road) is a self-contained place, a place you wouldn't visit without a purpose, a bustling, busy place where you get on with things, a place of no pretensions. You buy your new sweeping brush or your

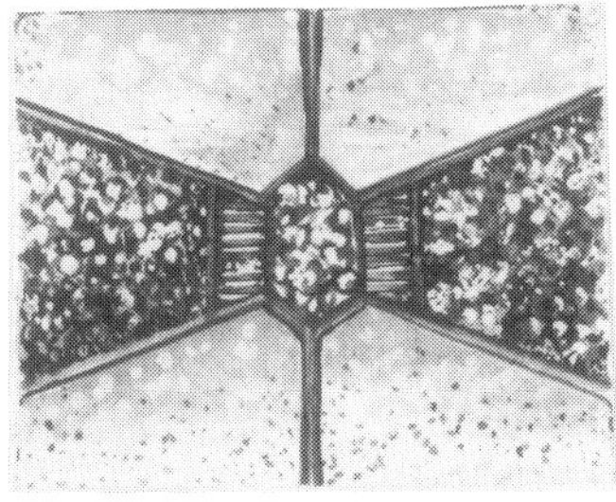

tap washer and hurry home to do something useful with it before the rarefied high altitude air gets to you. You can buy practically anything in Crookes, in a no-nonsense atmosphere that suggests perhaps 1947 (and long may it do so). The window of the sweet shop on the right is as you pass probably still crammed with screwtop jars full of Black Bullets and Sugar Fishes and Pineapple Pips and Wee Nippies and Alphabetical Letters and Rainbow Crystals (and Army and Navy Tablets). Forty years of British child tooth decay in one colouring-book display. On the left of this main road, until the mid-1980s, stood an institution whose loss was as sad as the demolition of

a medieval guildhall – Scott's Library, one of the city's last circulating libraries, where sixpence on the counter would buy you a breathless week with Sleeping Desire or Forbidden Flame or Caribbean Encounter or a thousand other Romances in sticky plastic covers. But at least there are still shops up here where you can take your football pools to be collected. The home fires are still burning.

At St Thomas's Church (3) on the right, glance at the pleasant village green churchyard behind the spiked gates. At the far end, under the spreading sycamore tree, the gravestone of William Johnson (died 1856) and his family packs in a whole Golden Treasury of verse. Back onto Crookes, cross and go down Coombe Road, turn right into Blakeney Road, where Nos 57 and 59 (Casa Los Arcos and its neighbour) have joined forces for a triumphal arched gateway of stone and wrought-iron – home improvement at its most spectacular. At the end, follow the cobbled alley (4) and, over the wall on the left, behold as stunning a panorama as Sheffield can offer. Over the playing fields is the city centre, its perspectives jam-packed, with the Town Hall tower nestling in Park Hill Flats, and the redbrick Firth Hall tower all but

disappearing under the slope (Sheffield's ever-varied heights often mean that only the top floors of tower blocks are visible from over the hill brows). Significantly, though, this is possibly the only place in Sheffield from which you can't see Shirecliffe College.

At the end of the alley, before crossing Crookes Road and heading up Lydgate Lane, glance right at the house with two eye-like windows in its end wall. As soon as you reach Lydgate Lane, turn left into Hallamgate Road where, with dislocating suddenness, brick terraces become stone Edwardian villas, leafy and faintly bohemian and universally prosperous and exactly what John Betjeman had in mind when he wrote his celebrated essay about Broomhill. The district was, he enthused – and the phrase is traditionally quoted whenever Broomhill is mentioned in newspapers, on the radio, or in polite middle-brow company – "the prettiest suburb in England." That, for the record, was on Monday July 3rd, 1961, in The Daily Telegraph, in a piece ranging over the whole of Sheffield, and taking in a few early impressions of Park Hill Flats ("At first sight, terrifying and inhuman").

Such sights are far away on the horizon from the top of Hallamgate Road, full of the "gabled black stone houses" (now cleaned up) about which Betjemen so rhapsodised, along with the "private cast-iron lamp posts that light the gravelled drives". Here they still are, as we turn left into Taptonville Road, where the stone walls balloon and bulge and pagoda-peaked summer houses and greenhouses with their own weather vanes perch on the lawns (and burglar alarms perch on the walls). Round cobbled Taptonville Crescent (5), its rhododendrons gently lit by gas lamps, and down to Fulwood Road, where Broomhill bustles in a higglepiggle of shops that leaves you little time or space to take in the gracious first floor windows over Fulwood Road Market. The first and

CAFE

second floors of Victorian rows of shops generally survive intact, whatever indignities have been foisted upon their ground floors.

Turn right, avoiding the bank and pub on their commanding brass-and-booze corner sites, and the scene spreads bracingly out as though we were already on the open road to Manchester. Left for a detour down Ashgate Road, where, opposite the severe white-painted Georgian houses gazing wide-eyed and unblinking at the light, Summerfield (6) hides behind the gate on the right. Cross this elegant Londonish square, where two blocks of shallow bay windows and half-glazed doors and the odd fire escape are tucked so neatly away and, at the other side, turn right onto Ashdell Road. Follow it steeply back onto Fulwood Road, turn left and (what a zigzag) left again onto Endcliffe Crescent, and then bear right all the time. An impressive paddock (7) opens out in the centre of this 1820s private estate, once – like so much of Broomhill and Broomhall – privately gated. The houses, now mostly occupied by students, are almost invisible behind the ivy-clad trees and wrought-iron gates. Follow the crescent road to the left, trying very hard to ignore the landscape blight of Sorby Hall, and turn left down the path next to the cricket nets.

Right onto the driveway and, at the gate, left into Endcliffe Vale Road. To the right is Endcliffe Hall, now a Territorial Army headquarters but once a grand industrialist's home where a tunnel was reputedly built so cattle being driven across the grounds could be channelled through without offending the master's view from his windows. Turn right into Riverdale Road, sedate suburbia in stone, and follow it down until, as it curves to the right, a gap in the wall opens into Endcliffe Park, here a narrow spurt of green between two roads, where the atmosphere is always Sunday afternoon. Bear left down the path and across the field beside the lake into Endcliffe Wood, part of Sheffield's 6,000 acres of woodland – seven per cent of the city area and over one million mature trees, making this one of the most wooded cities in Britain. Keep to the top of the high bank, glancing through the trees to the right at the monolith (8) commemorating Queen Victoria's Jubilee. It was originally erected in Town Hall Square in 1887 and moved here in 1905 to make way for the Queen's statue, which subsequently followed it in 1930 (Read on to Walk B).

Down towards the stepping stones is the quiet monument (9) to the ten American airmen who died when their Flying Fortress aircraft crash-landed here on February 22nd, 1944. Damaged by German bombers, the plane – one of 11 to come down over Sheffield during the Second World War – limped back to England where the pilot heroically managed to avoid Endcliffe's houses and children playing in the park. A wreath is laid every year and remains there, throughout the four seasons, until it is renewed. Finally, cross the stepping stones over the River Porter and three choices open out. Either left through the park to Hunter's Bar for the 81/2/3/4 or 33 buses back to the city centre, or to start Walk B, or across the field and up Ecclesall Road through Banner Cross to Walk C.

Around Hunter's Bar

Approximate distance: 1½ miles
Start: Buses Nos 81/2/3/4 or 33 from city centre to Hunter's Bar

Most surprisingly, Queen Victoria (1) stands with her back to Endcliffe Park, perhaps not amused by ordinary people's amusement. From her vantage point next to an oak tree planted for the coronation of her grandson, George V, she gazes out of the park with all the stone sternness befitting (as it says on the plinth) "A Great Queen". She had pride of Sheffield place in Town Hall Square from 1905 to 1930, when she was regally motored out to the suburbs one bright Sunday morning. The crown – apparently her only movable part – was lifted from her head and it was discovered that her two-and-a-half-ton statue stood on its fifty ton base without bolts or screws to secure it. Now we follow her gaze, in the opposite direction to the verdantly view-strewn Round Walk, for a couple of miles through Victorian Sheffield – where the lady's subjects were housed, alive and dead.

The first of many criss-crossings of the Porter Brook (we shall be up and down both sides of its valley) takes us left up and across Brocco Bank, and right into the grounds of St. Augustine's Church (2), a grand 1897 piece of Diamond Jubilee Ecclesiastical very high indeed on the Sheffield jumble sales Top Ten list. Look back over the hillside of slate and tile roofs clattering down from Psalter Lane, continue along a deceptively rural path, and turn left into Botanical Road, with its solid stone houses, all bay windows and laurels. The high wall of the Botanical Gardens curves up over the hill and, here as in many places on our walk, there's the sense of a country

Walk B:

1
BROCCO BANK
2
BOTANICAL RD
3
4
CLARKEHOUSE ROAD
PARK LANE
5
COLLEGIATE CRES.
ECCLESALL ROAD
10
9
8
SHARROW VALE ROAD
7
6
CEMETERY AVE.
CEMETERY ROAD

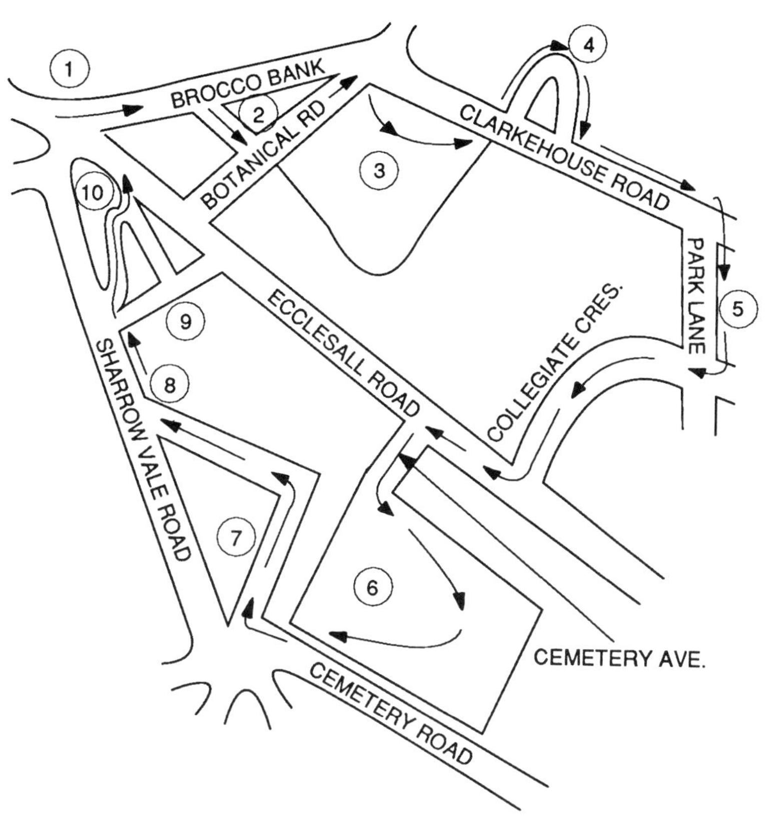

backwater somehow preserved near the very heart of a (post-)industrial city.

Over the hill and into the Botanical Gardens (3) at its wrought-iron turnstile. The Paxton pavilions – three miniature 1837 Crystal Palaces – are the most transparently Victorian features of Sheffield's little urban paradise (Ball Games not encouraged), with its twenty south-facing, and very select, acres and its 5,000 plants, each labelled, as the educationally improving Victorians would hope, in botanical Latin. Cornus controversa, pulmonaria augustifolia, skimmia rubella – not notifiable diseases, but species proud to thrive and be labelled in

this most civilised and cultivated of public parks, where Man has tamed Nature so immaculately . . . except in the Friends of the Earth Garden on the far side, where Nature is once more being allowed a bit of free rein.

A bear-pit to the right – best in Europe, they say – and a fossilised tree down the main avenue, 300 million years old and discovered during coal mining on the site of Midland Station. It grips the ground alongside the Crimean War Memorial (Victory not Victoria is enthroned up there), but we head past the pavilions, nodding to the shrieking macaws and picking our way through sunbathers and squirrels – and turn left at the notice-board (Ways to Keep Your Slugs Down) through the main gateway, a Sheffield Arc de Triomphe, a gateway making an officially approved, rubber-stamped statement and designed with rotund processions in mind.

We turn right across Clarkehouse Road, in the lowest reaches of Broomhill, the tree-lined haven of Sheffield's Victorian commuters. And we make a looping detour round Rutland Park (4) – professional and fashionable and elegant, a crescent where nannies with discreetly hooded perambulators should still lurk among the hydrangeas. Left again at the end of the crescent and past King Edward VII school, Sheffield's stately home of education.

Turn right into Park Lane (5) as it heads down a rural hill. To the left, Antrim Avenue and Park Crescent are full of unexpected lawns and stained glass windows and gracious iron gateways in swooning swirls. Past Broomhill Cottage, a yodelling Tyrolean fantasy, and right into Collegiate Crescent for the descent to Ecclesall

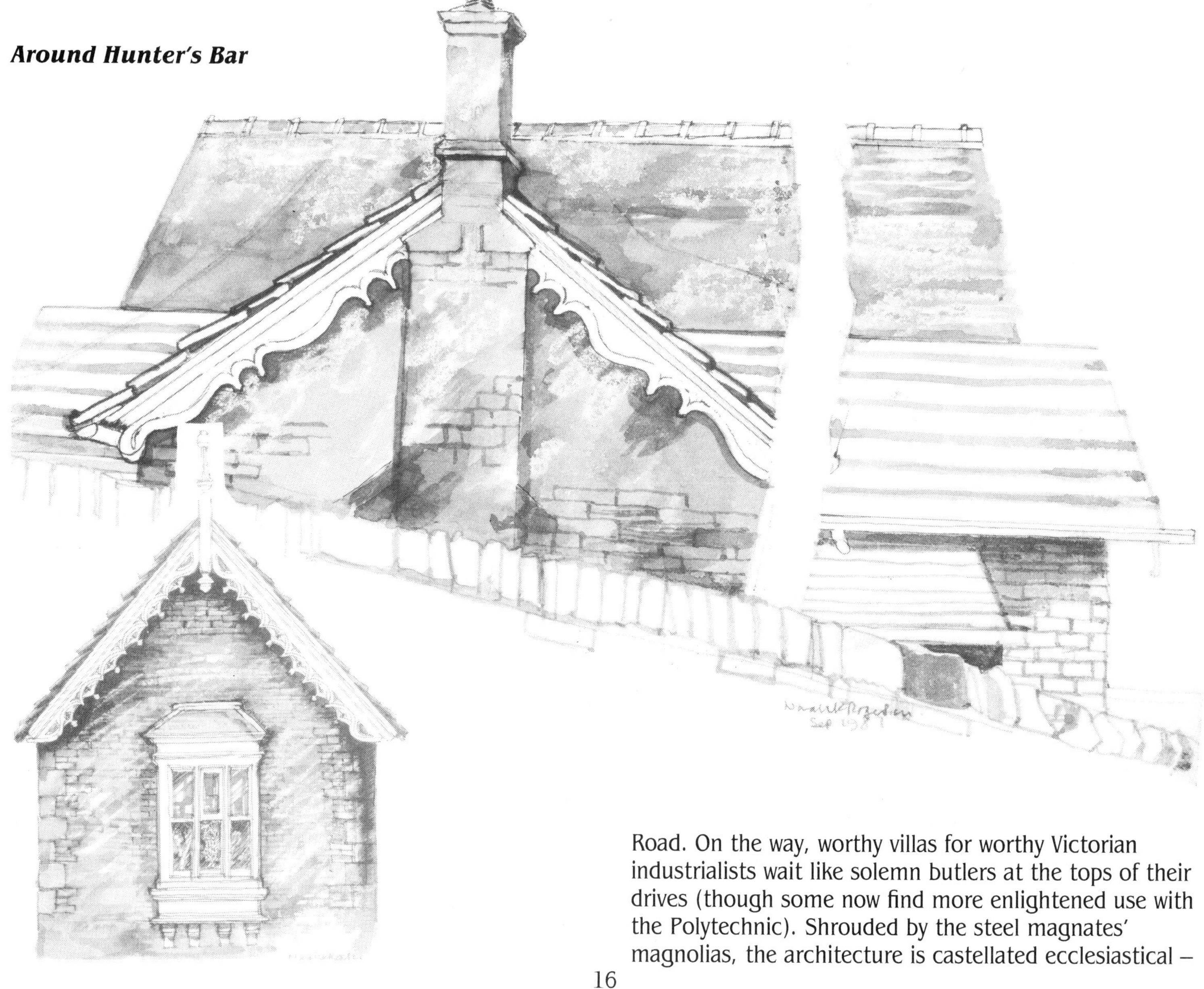

Road. On the way, worthy villas for worthy Victorian industrialists wait like solemn butlers at the tops of their drives (though some now find more enlightened use with the Polytechnic). Shrouded by the steel magnates' magnolias, the architecture is castellated ecclesiastical –

turrets and gables and dormers, all battlements and shields and bell-pulls and sentry box porches and medieval-looking stone heads that hint of grand family ancestry. And a quaintly ramshackle extension props itself against the house at the far end of the Victoria Road tennis courts.

Right into Ecclesall Road, left along the ceremonially straight trim terrace of Cemetery Avenue and, beneath the grinning lion gateway, into the General Cemetery (6). Here is Victorian death in all its grandeur – 20,000 graves at one time, 77,000 burials (very economical, the Victorians), a century and a half of hand-chiselled piety. Large areas of the once gloriously overgrown cemetery have recently been cleared to create a pleasant park, but the most interesting section, with the great monuments to wealthy grief, is being preserved around the 1836 Old Chapel. It includes, delightfully, Amor Spoor (d. 1865: "In life respected, in death lamented": no Victorian could ask for more) and, significantly, Samuel Holberry, the ill-fated Sheffield Chartist.

Holberry, one of Sheffield's First Eleven working-class folk heroes, died in prison, his stone laments, "at the early age of twenty-seven for advocating what to him appeared to be the true interest of the people of England". Some 50,000 of those people lined his 1842 funeral procession – a tribute to the popularity of his People's Charter for parliamentary reform and his plot to seize the Town Hall. It was, his court decided, an act of "seditious conspiracy" which has ironically ended with a commemorative plaque on the modern Town Hall extension.

Meanwhile, back in the General Cemetery, some of the headstones, with their patiently mourning cherubs, have been preserved. Others are laid (insensitively?) as a pathway, so from the gate take the middle path, running underneath the stone arcade, and pick your way reverently over the Mauds and the Ebenezers and the Septimi. Just past the horse–chestnut tree is the gravestone of Margaret Green – a touching testament to Victorian infant mortality. She lost ten children in nineteen years – all are listed, their ages ranging from six days to seven years. When Mrs. Green herself joined them, she was simply remembered: "She was brought as a lamb to the slaughter".

At the end of the path, go down the steps and head up towards the church-like 1848 New Chapel. Just beneath it, the stone of Hannah Snidal is half-embedded in a tree trunk (and this "after an illness of only 57 hours"). And on the steep, stony path, Ralph Barber, we read approvingly, bequeathed £500 to "Aged, destitute, unmarried females". Turn right at the New Chapel, up the

hill, and through the ornate 1836 Egyptian gateway with its serpents circling into wreaths and biting their own tails for the sheer decorative joy of it. And so up Cemetery Road (or back down through the Cemetery towards the city centre, emerging at Montague Street, straight ahead and right onto Ecclesall Road as far as Summerfield Street, to start Walk D through Broomhall).

Assuming you're still here, at the highest point of Cemetery Road, by the solid green gas lamp, turn right for the steep, dark, damp and mossy descent along Frog Walk (7). Left at the bottom, along Toad Walk (T'owd Walk) by the Porter, and past the idyllic mill-pond scene at Wilsons' Snuff Mill (8), a separate company since an 1831 family tiff from J & H Wilson, also snuff, just up the hill in its more austere Westbrook Mill. Wilsons, the mill-pond ones, have been making their nose-tingling, finger-staining, waistcoat-showering snuff in much the same way since 1737 – Jock's Choice and Tonquin and Jockey Club and Crumbs of Comfort. Their eighteenth century waterwheel is reckoned the oldest piece of working machinery in Europe and their private list still bristles with field marshals, judges, admirals and bishops – perhaps thanks to a secret ingredient kept locked and bolted in Room Thirty-Nine and divulged only to two members of each generation of the family. On still afternoons, the aroma of snuff percolates provocatively over Sharrow Vale Road.

Onto which we turn right. A Hansel and Gretel cottage with hinged shutters poses picturesquely on the right and, a few steps up Hickmott Road, the red corrugated iron Wycliffe Independent Church (9), built at the turn of the century, shows a nicely practical outlook on worship. The riverside site could not support a heavy all-brick building plus packed congregation when the church first opened as Independent Protestant. The Wycliffites took it over with an auspiciously timed inaugural service – on VE Day 1945 – and its most celebrated incumbent, the Rev

'Daddy' Vince, is still remembered for his fondness for driving around in an old fire engine with his beard blowing in the wind.

Next right on Sharrow Vale Road, alongside the Porter Cottage Pub, is the prettily curving Meadow Terrace (10), all cobbles and window boxes and hanging baskets, like a little bit of Brighton brought up North. Left into Neill Road and on to Hunter's Bar for a final reproving welcome back from Queen Victoria. From here, take the 81/2/3/4 or 33 bus back to the city centre, or walk up Ecclesall Road through Banner Cross for walk C.

Brincliffe to Heeley

Approximate distance: 3 miles
Start: Buses Nos 81/2/3/4 from city centre to Banner Cross

Go forward through Banner Cross with two glances back. On the steep hill of Ecclesall Road from Hunter's Bar, glance back first over the deepest green panorama of deepest Blue Hallam – the busky backdrop of Ranmoor where only the very tallest gable makes itself seen through the trees. Then glance back in history to Charlie Peace, celebrated Sheffield criminal who murdered the husband of a woman he claimed was his lover at their home – No 959 Ecclesall Road (1) – in 1876. The house has been converted into a shop – like much of Banner Cross, whose former residential character is signalled only by the stone house names over the shop fronts: Bannerdale Villa, Brentwood Villa, Marlbro (too long for full name) Villa. Banner Cross and Greystones are particularly rich in these bourgeois names – even the humblest pair of terrace houses is likely to be ennobled as a memorial to the Empire as Mafeking or Pretoria Villas.

Carry on up Ecclesall Road, peer down Glenalmond Road, whose fronts are bright and fussy enough for seaside boarding houses, and cross Psalter Lane. On the right is a picturesque early nineteenth century cottage – white-washed and mullioned and churchified; a Barchester sort of place which, uprooted to the Shire counties, would fetch a fortune as a second home. Turn left up Brincliffe Edge Road, whose suburban bay windows reflect every Welfare State grammar school boy's ambition – a safe job, a nice wife, and a Dungroanin semi at Bents Green or Ecclesall. Climb the hill, perhaps venturing (left after Quarry Lane) into the hidden park around Brincliffe Towers (2), an old people's home with as grand a set of mock-Tudor chimneys as you'll see anywhere in Sheffield.

Back on the road, trees hem in overhead until, at the crest of the ridge, a top of the world vista reveals most of Sheffield on the left and, on the right, through the silver birchwood, most of Millhouses. Amazing to have so many semi-detached houses in one place. And so many Venetian blinds. Past a house called Wit's End, the early Victorian atmosphere is very strong – tight, shuttered homes the Brontes would have liked. Opposite a lamp post squeezed into the wall, turn left down Union Road for a straight descent into leaf-packed Nether Edge. Sheffield's roads are lined by 15,000 trees – and on a bright sunny day most of them seem to be here in Nether Edge. Beechy seclusion is the keynote, a cosy stone-built sense of a quiet community as you pass the grandly gated drive of Nether Edge Hospital on the left, cross Osborne Road and carry on up Cherry Tree Road for the beechiest, most secluded part of all – Meadow Bank Avenue (3) on the right. Promenade graciously through this most elegant of Sheffield backwaters and at the far end take the steep cobbled path down the hill (so very rural) into Machon Bank Road.

Here, past the tunnel of trees on Montgomery Road, is the bustling heart of Nether Edge (Nether Edge Market, a stone sign over the shops proclaims, ferns curling round it). Turn into Moncrieffe Road and immediately right down Machon Bank, where the houses, with individual

Walk C:

ECCLESALL ROAD
1
PSALTER LANE
2
BRINCLIFFE EDGE ROAD
UNION ROAD
CHERRY TREE ROAD
OSBORNE ROAD
3
MACHON BANK RD.
MONCRIEFFE RD.
MACHON BANK
ABBEYDALE RD.
LITTLE LONDON ROAD
BROADFIELD ROAD
4
BEDALE ROAD
CHESTERFIELD ROAD
5
MEERSBROOK PARK ROAD
VALLEY ROAD
LONDON ROAD
6
WELL ROAD
ARTISAN VIEW
7
GLEADLESS ROAD
8
GUERNSEY RD.
ALDERSON ROAD
SHARROW LANE
LONDON ROAD
WOODHEAD ROAD
10
9
BRAMALL LANE

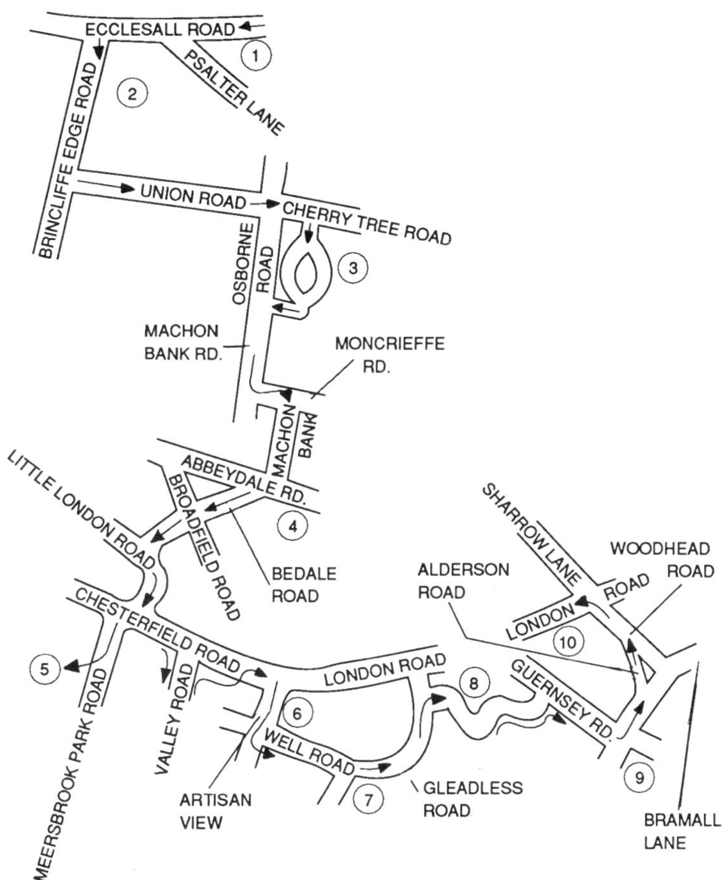

CINEMA
A & F DRAKE LTD
office equipment

motifs on their doorposts, are quaintly stepped round an inconvenient corner. Nature abhors a straight line; the Victorians abhorred a curve. At the bottom, the great white whale of the Abbeydale Cinema (4) looms into view. A people's palace on the brow of the hill with gently curving front, with towers and dome and, in its heyday, with tubes of fluorescent light cascading in waterfalls. Opened in 1920, closed in 1975, now an office equipment showroom, but still boasting its nymphs and lions' heads and cherubs doing odd things with bunches of grapes, and its fire curtains with adverts for The Raincoat Shop (Remember We Sell Nothing Else) and Brentano – Everything For Making Lampshades. And still boasting, of course, its smoky, light-flickering memories.

Cross Abbeydale Road and bear right down steep Bedale Road, then straight ahead along the path to the right of the River Sheaf, where a single massive black gatepost stands as forlorn as a prehistoric stone. Left onto Little London Road and follow the curve right, past the elegant two-storeyed frontage of Tyzack Turners' Works, under the railway bridge, across Chesterfield Road and up Meersbrook Park Road for (astonishingly) Meersbrook Park (5).

A curious park, Meersbrook – the steepest, most unrelentingly steepest, of Sheffield's forty-eight parks, where the city ethic is made turf. You don't idle away your time here, like you might in some effete southern park. You work, and work hard, even on a Sunday stroll. Football matches are possible here only between players with one leg longer than the other. As you pick-axe your way to the top, the grandest of views opens out over the allotments, with the greenness of Fulwood gradually weeded out to the concrete creamness of the city centre and the red brickness beyond. Perching at the very top is Bishops' House, an unexpected outcrop of 1500 half-timbering. Not a bishops' residence at all, but once the home of the Blythe family, two of whose members became bishops (of Lichfield and Coventry). Now a museum full of curious corners and curious beams to bang your head on. Through the copse is Meersbrook Hall, the four-square 1780 headquarters of the council's recreation department that enjoyed a sixty-year celebrity as second home (from 1890 to 1953) of the Ruskin Museum. The original museum – Victorian art historian John Ruskin's treasure-house of cultural clutter – was in Walkley, but it was here at Meersbrook that the collection achieved international fame. American visitors are reputed to have sailed to England specifically to kneel in front of Ruskin's bust and kiss the floor where his feet would have been. Just across the hill is a trim marble fountain (no water now) "erected by the members of the British United Order of Oddfellows" to William Westram. Among its scrolls and flowers is a fine bit of Victorian opportunism – the masons, Eatons, carved their full business address (529 Intake Road) on the most prominent pillar.

Back down to Meersbrook Park Road, where generations of Whit Walks have unfurled their billowing banners, and retrace your steps to Chesterfield Road. Right and down the hill, pausing perhaps in Valley Road on the right to admire the fine fortified frontage of Tyzacks Meersbrook Works – prim sycamore leaves on the pillars and a single, rather dainty first floor bay window to break the symmetry. Back on London Road (as Chesterfield Road has become) a horse trough used to stand in the broad-arched recess on the left, but we head hurriedly down to Artisan View (6) where the White Lion pub has ingeniously squeezed a plaster advert for Gilmours Windsor Ales and Stouts on its end gable.

John Shortridge's works at Attercliffe

Artisan View – wonderfully Heeley. A hard slog all the way and a blank end when you get there – a neat summing up of the life of your average artisan. Heeley was once a major centre for Sheffield knife and toolmaking – Little Sheffield, they called it. Now most of its back-to-backs have been demolished to leave a grassy hillside, and the artisans' view over Sheffield and the high dark moors over Ringinglow is less hemmed-in than it used to be. View Road and Prospect Road are the names here, with much justification.

Turn left onto Well Road and carry on past cobbled streets as melancholy as Roman roads (the names of Oak Street and the rest are still in the street guides) to St Andrew's Primitive Methodist Church (7), impossibly imposing in its Acropolis isolation. A remarkably symmetrical 1895 building, this, big enough to seat every Methodist in Heeley, primitive or otherwise. Foundation stone, it says, laid by the Mayor, Charles Thomas Skelton, whose Sheafbank toolworks (estab 1855) spreads out from the bottom of Gleadless Road. Skelton, mayor at a time when Sheffield's municipal leaders were automatically its captains of industry, could gaze down from his church to his factory and reflect that, despite the back-to-backs between them, everything was right in God's world.

Up Gleadless Road, past the equally imposing Ann's Road School (big arches and spiked gateways) are an 1820 Methodist Chapel and Heeley Parish Church, with its obelisk to John Shortridge. If the lettering hadn't been eroded by the high winds of Heeley, it might say that Shortridge was a Victorian builder and engineer

(he built the Wicker Arches) whose home, Chipping House, in Chippinghouse Road, was named (quite logically) after Chipping, the Lancashire village where his wife was born. It reputedly took twenty horses to drag his memorial's granite base up here.

Down Gleadless Road and, before the 1758 chapel, which satisfied the Primitive Methodists until they moved proudly up the hill, bear right at the Sheaf View pub and follow Cutlers Walk (8) as it zigzags along the River Sheaf. Past Skeltons factory on the right—famed for its manure forks, the sign says—and the high railway embankment on the left and the graffiti (Terry and Karen and Dickie and Punk Rules and, enigmatically, History), then over the bridge and through the tunnel under the railway and out along the cobbled gennel to Guernsey Road (by-passing Heeley Bottom, no longer at its best as a Grand Prix racing track).

Right onto Queens Road where Havelock Bridge is dominated by Monks 1868 plaster sign (9) and (glancing right) Sheffield's highest wall on Prospect Road. Cross to Bramall Lane, where the collective intake of breaths – the roar of Oohs and Aaahs – echoes through Saturday afternoons, and left at Alderson Road. Left again at Woodhead Road and onto London Road and left past Victoria Buildings and Albert Buildings with a glimpse right up Sharrow Lane at Mount Pleasant, the stark 1777 home of the Sitwells that has served as lunatic asylum, school for foundling girls, driving school, social security office and now community centre (a fine Adam ceiling inside). Here, in the multicultural inner city bazaar of Highfield, be inspired or improved by the quotation from Thomas Carlyle between the pair of one-armed Muses over the door of Highfield Library (10): "That there should be one man die ignorant who had capacity for knowledge, this I call a tragedy." Inspired or improved, take a 17/24/75/76 bus back to the city centre or turn up Sharrow Lane, right onto Washington Road and down Summerfield Street to Walk D.

Broomhall and Portobello

Approximate distance: 1 mile
Start: Buses Nos 81/2/3/4 or 33 from city centre to Summerfield Street

A wander tempting you off the straight and wide, round byways rather than highways, from almost suburban to defiantly urban, residential to industrial and post-industrial. Up back lanes, alleys, snickets and gennels, many quiet and picturesque in a built-up way and all hinting at the character of the city before the motorcar ruled every planning decision. Some are a little shabby, a touch run-down – they are too busy adapting to changing patterns of work (or lack of it) to worry about looking pretty. On the way we meet buildings proudly bearing some of the great names of Sheffield citylore.

We start on Ecclesall Road opposite the end of Summerfield Street and take the steps up the hill – the site of a group of elegant Victorian houses demolished in the early 1970s for a traffic scheme that was never put into action. Now the slope is dominated by Sunny Bank nature reserve, a project launched by Sheffield City Wildlife Group in 1987 and offering a multi-coloured summer carpet of poppies, cornflowers, rose bay willow herb and dandelions (rehabilitated as wild flowers rather than weeds).

Go straight ahead along Broomhall Place, site on the right of an 1834 neo-classical terrace which was demolished in 1985 amid considerable controversy. Turn right into Broomhall Street and, beyond St Silas' Church, right again into Hanover Square (1). Here you have it – urban regeneration, an 1800 square, with a cobbled carriage turn, rescued from genteel but seedy decay. Until the early 1980s, it was a silted backwater of the inner city, suffering from Broomhall's red light reputation and choked by a jungle of overgrown undergrowth. Its fifteen houses had escaped demolition in the 1950s (they were to be replaced by more manageable maisonettes) and, with Collinsons Dancing School in prime position, it sank slowly into the bohemian moss smothering its cobbles. The Beet family had owned it since 1891 and occupied three of the houses, but with rents as low as £120 a year little could be done in the way of upkeep and they sold the square for £30,000 to the South Yorkshire Housing Association who spent ten times that amount on renovation. The rescue has left the square cleaner and lighter and its atmosphere will probably return in time – though the closeness of Hanover Flats peeping over the wall at the end doesn't really help.

Glance across the dual carriageway at another site – Viners cutlery factory – double back along Broomhall Street and turn right into Wharncliffe Road. Pause at Collegiate Crescent and consider the difference between Broomhall and Broomhill. Their names differ by only one letter, their ideologies by a lexicon. The Hill has become a Citroen-owning ghetto of yuppie/drabbieness; the Hall is regenerating multi-ethnic inner-city – until you come to Collegiate Crescent, a sort of Checkpoint Muesli.

Turn left for a glimpse of old Broomhall Park, a carefully planned, carefully preserved, once carefully gated early Victorian stone-built estate. On the left are Mackenzie Crescent (2) and, a little farther up, though you could easily miss it, Wilton Place. Their steeply-gabled, rather prim and proper houses cluster round

Walk D:

9
10
TRIPPET LANE
8
ST. GEORGE'S TERRACE
PORTOBELLO
LEAVY GREAVE
VICTORIA
7
ST.
6
5
GLOSSOP ROAD
CONVENT
WALK
3
4
WILKINSON ST
FILEY ST.
HOLBERRY CL.
WHARNCLIFFE ROAD
COLLEGIATE CR.
BROOMHALL ST
1
2
SUNNY BANK
ECCLESALL ROAD

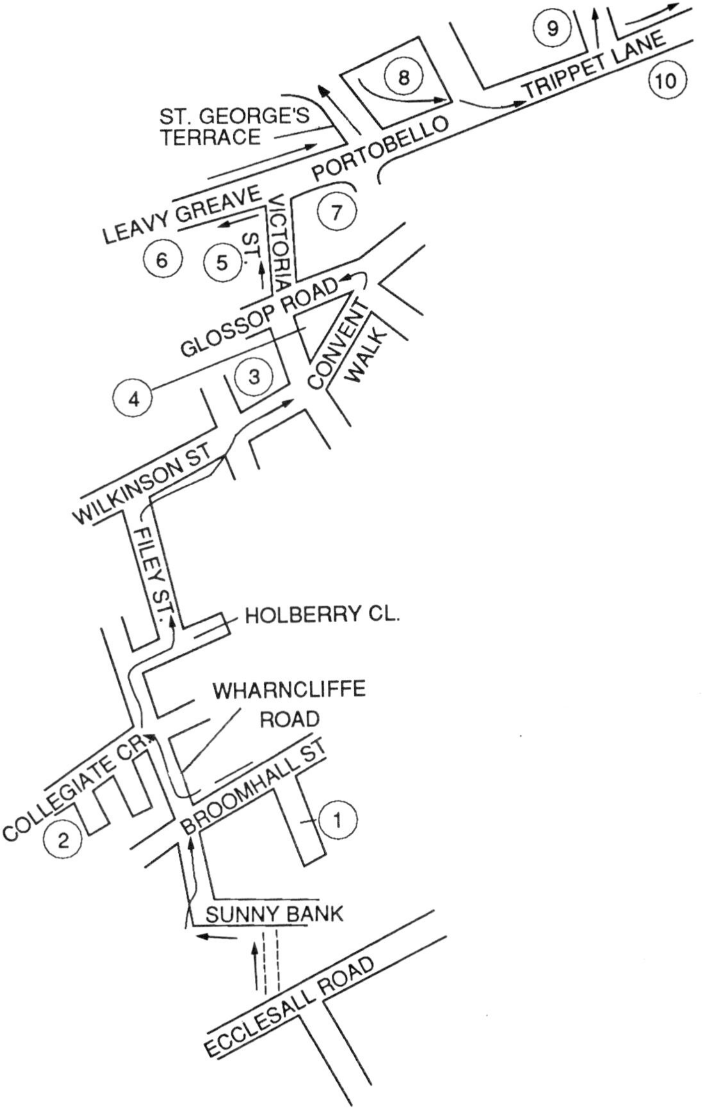

grassed carriage loops – little Hanover Squares, havens of taste with books and cats in every window. Thackeray's characters would have been more than happy here.

Return to the crossroads and turn left into Brunswick Street, noting the rather bored looking medievalish heads on the university nursery ("Quiet please, children sleeping") and right into Holberry Close, the ideological renaming of Havelock Square. Left up Filey Street, with its genteel wrought-iron balconies and its square ground floor bays oddly contrasted with rounded first floor windows. Past more bored medieval heads on Hanover Methodist Church (two buildings oddly linked by a vast stained glass window) – and at the top turn right into

Wilkinson Street, one of Sheffield's most unexpectedly elegant roads. Cross (carefully) the dual carriageway and opposite No 9 (3) note the early nineteenth century iron triangular boundary mark, a relic of an administrative township system that lasted from the late middle ages until 1900 and followed the old field lines. This one marks the division between Nether Hallam and Sheffield – and others nestle in Western Bank (just down from the main university building) and Carver Street (junction with Division Street – See Walk E).

At the end of Wilkinson Street, take the alley to the right of the car park past the Bath Hotel, a trim, spick and span, rather nautical affair with a stylishness few Sheffield pubs aspire to. Uprooted to Henley on Thames, it would hardly look out of place as the focal point for a regatta. Straight ahead is Convent Walk, alongside Glossop Road Baths (4), a building so day-to-day familiar it's easy not to notice the decorative neatness of its 1898 cream and red brickwork, the grandeur of its tower (it wouldn't disgrace Florence on a rainy day) and the extravagance of its carved stonework – proving decisively that for the Victorians bathing could be almost as worthy an activity as worshipping or banking.

To the right on Cavendish Street is Notre Dame School, a darkly Dickensian building with a Gothic air and the Virgin Mary flanked by angels over the door. But (unless you want to turn right onto Fitzwilliam Street and left onto Devonshire Street for Walk E across the city centre) turn left and left again onto Glossop Road and right up Victoria Street where the squat 1858 Church of the Nazarene (5) (Born Again Wesleyan Evangelical, since

Samuel Plimsoll's house

you ask) is one of the few in Britain with both a bell tower and a spire. At the top of Victoria Street glance to the left down Leavygreave at Hendersons' Relish factory (6). No great architectural gem but, perhaps as much as Viners, it has taken Sheffield's name all over the world. Hendersons, with its Belisha orange labelled bottles, is a sort of Worcester Sauce. Though only sort of. For over a century (the history is vague) it has infiltrated its exotic ingredients – tamarind and cloves and garlic and cayenne pepper – into homes serving nothing more exciting than steak and kidney pie. Half a million bottles a year are shipped out from the back shed (where the staff canteen seats four) to ex-pat Sheffielders all over the colonies. But strangely Hendersons is a delicacy hardly available in England north of Barnsley or south of Alfreton.

Right at Leavygreave and glance down Regent Terrace where Harrisons' plum-painted frontage (7) proclaims, in letters you wouldn't disagree with, "Steeplejack of Nelson Column fame". Estab 1854, this is Sheffield's oldest firm of steeplejacks with its natty slogan Height for Hire. Teddy Harrison, the second of five generations of his family, was the first man to climb Nelson's Column, the Everest of civic stonework. In 1896, he was commissioned to decorate it with seven and a half tons of flowers and to give the admiral the once-over. Arm badly fractured below the biceps, he noted.

Cross Portobello, once a thriving centre of cutlery making (still the occasional works sign) and follow St George's Terrace, alongside the Jessop Hospital, to glimpse, across on the left, Butler's Cafe, a very Hendersons' Relish sort of place. Again nothing much as architecture, but everything as folklore (famed for its meat and potato pie). Four generations of Butlers have catered here in their workers' cafe since 1910 – for the Sheffield Regent Cycling Club and the Darnall Kennel Association and the Sheffield Association of Billiards Club League. Butlers was the place where former council leader George Wilson, in the days of fob-watched municipal Socialism, would take reporters for a mug of tea. A truly bohemian place with its weathered cream plaster and its Park Drive adverts, where Little Mesters and university lecturers shared boiled turbot and college pudding and the occasional Small Tripe Supper. Picasso ate here during the 1950 World Council for Peace and drew a dove on a napkin, subsequently auctioned, now lost.

On the right (8) is St George's Church (1821), once grimly black, now cream-clean, and with a churchyard including (at the junction of St George's Terrace and Brook Hill) a tomb with a tune. Benjamin Coldwell (died 1868), owner of a lime and plaster works, had his passage to heaven serenaded by the hymn carved complete with music along the side of the tomb: "Great God! What do I see here! The end of things created!" The exclamatory immediacy of the verse is matched only by the inscription on the tall, very slim monument to Mary Holroyd, where piety has been desperately squeezed in:

"She was but words are
Wanting to say what!
Think what a wife should
Be and she was that."

Back into Portobello Street, alongside the grand and

handsome University Department of Applied Science, past the Sheffield Assay Office – one of only four in the country where gold, silver and platinum are hallmarked – and along Trippet Lane for a brief detour down Bailey Lane. On the left, over a doorway, a pointer dog (9) stretches out nose and tail over the inscription Stanch – the Dog Brand trademark of J & Riley Carr, makers of saws and guillotine knives on the site until the late 1950s. On the corner of Trippet Lane and Holly Street, Walter Tricketts' 200-year-old Anglo Works (10) is a cutlery factory of traditional Sheffield design and traditional Sheffield working methods. Steep stone steps, big brass bell you punch with the palm of your hand . . . Tricketts once made the molecular structure of an atom in sterling silver as well as turning out lobster forks, cranberry sauce spoons and asparagus servers. Just to the right of the main building – at a Entrance Keep Clear sign – a steep cobbled alley (West Bank Lane) climbs the hill under a broken gas lamp. It is typical of the backyard huddle of small scale Sheffield cutlery, all rackety wooden

staircases and broken windows stuffed with old Morning Telegraphs and oddly sweet smells. Turn left past Ridal & Co Horn Merchants (the letters flaking off the crumbling doors) and, at the end of this urban ramble, you'll be very surprised indeed where you come out in the city off-centre (left and down Church Street incidentally for walk G or right and up West Street and down Eldon Street for Walk E).

Through the city centre

Approximate distance: 1½ miles
Start: Buses No 52 (briefly if necessary) from the city centre

Sheffield's shopping centre straggles north to south in a narrow band of merchandising from Lady's Bridge to the Manpower Services building, that Aztec pyramid of brick that brings The Moor to such a decisive full stop. But our walk crosses this axis west to east, taking in the traditional heart of the cutlery industry, before ending with one of the most honest panoramas of the city.

We start in Devonshire Street (1), on the corner of Broomhall Street, whose bottom end we encountered in Walk D. Demolition has split the street into three unconnected stretches, but it reaches a grand culmination at the former Wharncliffe Fire Clay Works, a riot of decorative stone detail – lilies and Renaissance artists and grim women garlanded with scrolls and leaves. No stone uncarved. Head along Devonshire Street towards the city centre and glance left up Westfield Terrace where the vast frontage of the 1834 Mount Zion Congregational Church (2) has been preserved, though the Royal Hospital, which used to embrace it, has been demolished. An architect could call the frontage Ionic, but the effect is somehow stunningly Egyptian. Cross Devonshire Street and turn down into Trafalgar Street, where the 1883 Aberdeen Works boasts – in a quiet way –

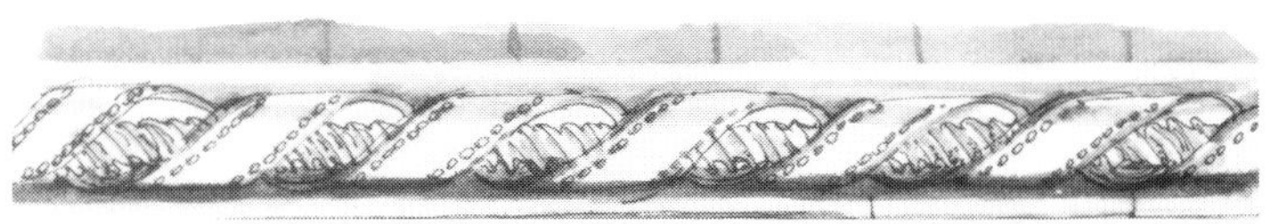

Walk E:

DEVONSHIRE STREET
BROOMHALL ST.
1
2
TRAFALGAR STREET
WESTFIELD TERRACE
DIVISION STREET
CARVER STREET
3
BARKERS POOL
4
TOWN HALL
CHARLES ST.
PATERNOSTER ROW
8
ARUNDEL ST.
7
SURREY ST.
5
NORFOLK STREET
SHOREHAM ST.
ARUNDEL GATE
6
TURNER ST.
LEADMILL RD.
MIDLAND STATION
GRANVILLE ST.
9
NORFOLK ROAD
10

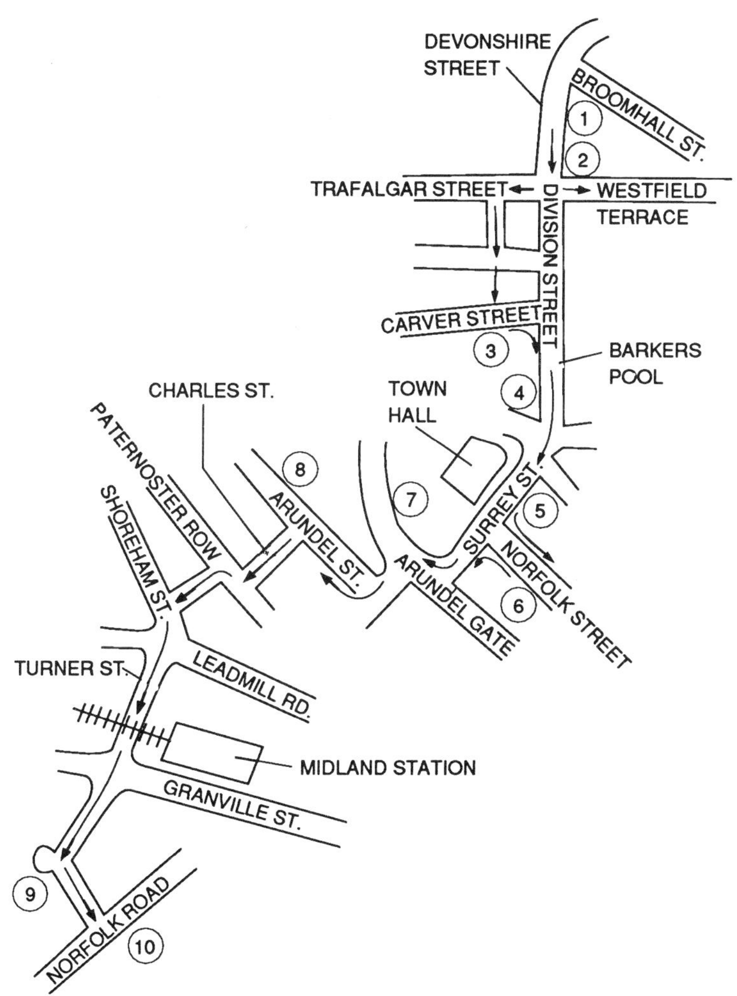

a classic Sheffield frontage. Left into Devonshire Lane for a relic (to the left up Canning Street) of humbler cutlery-making conditions: tumbledown tenements (though complete with elegantly elaborate door posts). Cross the car park behind the vast new fire station and, just above the bright red and green Staniforths sign, crammed down a narrow gable end, look inside St Matthew's Church (3). This 1854 Anglo-Catholic haven, with its bright white walls, stands alongside a main route long used by fire engines. On each pew is placed a card: "When the emergency services sirens pass outside the church, please pray 'For those who may be in danger in this incident' and 'For those who are hastening to help them'."

Turn up Carver Street where, at the Division Street junction, another township boundary marker lurks (see Walk D). Turn right towards Barker's Pool past the daunting array of classical heads over Cambridge House

(once the Sheffield Waterworks headquarters) and glance to the right down the darkly Dickensian Carver Lane with its packed workshops and the hemmed-in back of St Matthew's. For fifty years, Barker's Pool was dominated by the grotto-like entrance of the Gaumont Cinema (4), the grandest relic of Sheffield's golden age of picture houses. In 1931, the city had forty-five cinemas, with a total seating capacity of 36,000 . . . The Forum, Southey, and The Lyric, Darnall; The Capitol, Lane Top, and The Sunbeam, Pitsmoor; The Ritz, Parson Cross and, most

wondrously, the Walkley Palladium. (Death Defying Thrills! Breath-Taking Romances! Novelty Organ Interludes!). The Gaumont, opened as The Regent in 1927 with the latest Mary Pickford, was demolished in 1985 and replaced by the new Odeon Cinema. The scarlet greenhouse structure that surrounds it has caused keen controversy. Its imaginative but incongruous girder design contrasts oddly with the blandly blended stonework of the more bijou Orchard Square development opened in 1987 just across Leopold Street.

But we press on past the Town Hall, where Vulcan, perched atop his tower, turns his back on Sheffield's industrial East End and raises a fistful of arrows to salute the leafy Tory West. (It can't be long before he is moved around to a more ideologically sound alignment). The Town Hall's celebrated frieze of buffers and ivory-turners and electro-platers needn't distract from the gryphons and lions guarding the savings of the Yorkshire Bank's investors. The bank, once the Albany Hotel, rounds off Surrey Street, one of Sheffield's most homogeneous architectural units, with almost more Town Hall Gothic than the Town Hall itself can muster.

First on the left comes the Montgomery Theatre (5), the heartland of the city's amateur theatre-going, the home of Brigadoon and White Horse Inn and Wild Violets, where programme obituaries to veteran thespians declare: "Well-played to the final curtain!" The theatre is part of the Montgomery Hall, built in 1886 as a memorial to newspaper editor James Montgomery (we meet his statue on walk G). For years it was the headquarters of the Sunday School Union, letting off salvos against alcohol and greyhound racing and Sunday newspapers and horror comics, and laying on Whit Sings and free breakfasts for 'Street Arabs'. The perfect prelude to a theatre evening here with Roses Operatic has long been a Theatre Tea (in very capital letters) at Tuckwoods Restaurant next door. A very respectable place, Tuckwoods, Sheffield's oldest restaurant (estab 1856 in Fargate). When it secured its drinks licence in 1986 after forty sober years on its present site, it was like the Women's Institute starting evening classes in glue-sniffing. Tuckwoods has always been a Brief Encounterish sort of place, where honest meals of Jumbo Scampi and Small Mixed Grill and Large Mixed Grill and Steamed Treacle Sponge have long been served, with cutlery you have to lift with both hands, to old ladies in big hats. Giddy with sparkling non-alcoholic grape juice, they would stagger into the Montgomery for a riotous evening with The Arcadians. Town Hall clerks with ink-smudged suits would prop their plastic-backed library books on the solid silver condiments to recover from the heady excitement of spending Boots gift vouchers. When it was sited in Fargate, a Resting Room was provided for patrons to sleep off heavy meals.

Just along is Channing Hall, with its astonishingly rich tiled staircase, and, round the corner in Norfolk Street, the Jeffie Bainbridge Children's Shelter has its name

inscribed on scrolled stonework over a doorway on the left. Jeffie was the wife of philanthropist Emerson Bainbridge, who opened the shelter in her memory in 1894 as a sanctuary for Sheffield's needy children. In Norfolk Street are two further oases of peace. Outdoors, the Upper Chapel courtyard houses statues by the Sheffield-born sculptor George Fullard (thin Sheffielders in uncharacteristic repose – and his Walking Man strides out under the Town Hall extension). And indoors, across the road, is the Ruskin Gallery (6), an exquisite temple of cultural delight. Dedicated to Ruskin's aim of showing art to the artisans, giving them glimpses of European culture before package holidays and television made it widely accessible, the gallery is perhaps the only place in Sheffield where you will find people studying a lump of coal as a thing of beauty.

Back on to Surrey Street, past the Central Library, with fossils easily seen in its limestone, down the steps and right onto Arundel Gate, where the grass verge beside the subway features a memorial to Sheffield's most celebrated musician, Sir William Sterndale Bennett (7). Born in 1816 on the site, in a house on the corner of Howard Street and Norfolk Street, Sterndale Bennett's celebrity can be judged by the inscription on his mournfully bewhiskered bust in the Cathedral where the list of his musical honours tails off quickly into "etc, etc". Professor of Music at Cambridge, Principal of the Royal Academy of Music, Wagner's successor as conductor of the Philharmonic Society of London . . . he was dubbed "angel-musician" by Schumann, had his works conducted by Mendelssohn and was knighted four years before his 1875 death and burial in Westminster Abbey. His pleasantly conservative music, wildly admired by the Victorians, now languishes in dusty obscurity, perhaps because his inspiration faltered early. Still, at the age of five, he was playing the Hallelujah Chorus on the piano after hearing it just once, and he introduced cricket to Germany in the 1830s. Few can claim as much.

Under the subway, where the traffic noise would have terrified Sterndale Bennett, down Howard Street and right into Arundel Street, long a centre of the Sheffield cutlery industry. A 200 yard walk takes you through 200 years of Sheffield history, down narrow brick passages into dark yards. Around a hundred firms operate here now – many of them one-man affairs: men, perhaps, carrying on the work of the great-grandfathers. From Slater's Venture Works, the atmosphere seems little changed since the 1770s, when the street was part of a purpose-built grid. At its centre, at No 72, is the four-storey Butchers Works (8), whose archway opens into a cobbled yard straight out of Oliver Twist. Built around 1825, its blackened chimneys smoke, its wooden staircases zigzag up the walls, its pipes criss-cross and its stone steps are as steep as a cliff side. Its workshops are like little homes with their tables and chairs and wardrobes (and usually valve radios and pin-up calendars). Little homes with big furnaces.

Turn left down Charles Street, cross to Grinders Hill, left across Shoreham Street and across Leadmill Road to the right of the culvert where the River Porter surfaces briefly on its secret route through the city centre. Follow Turner Street, up the steps to the solidly riveted cast iron bridge over the railway (seen vertiginously through the gaps in the wooden planks). Stretching out to the left over the crazy paving of station roofs is the now desolate

Granville Street with surely the longest wall in Sheffield. Up the steps and diagonally left up more steps between the garages and at the top pause (you might as well – there is no path to lead you anywhere else). The view from Vulcan's thigh level pans round from Meersbrook to Shirecliffe via at least a dozen spires. A pop-up book of the city with the perspective crammed together.

But we are here to inspect the seventy foot Cholera Monument (9), an anorexic spire of stone commemorating the 402 Sheffield victims of Britain's 1832 cholera epidemic, buried here in a mass grave. Just behind it, away from the hoi-polloi, is the tomb of John Blake, the Master Cutler who was one of the victims of this "calamitous infliction." Turn left and follow the roses to the gateway where across Norfolk Road the 1825 Shrewsbury Almshouses (10) cluster in mock-Tudor cosiness round their courtyard. And from here either retrace your steps or turn left for a descent through the echoing concrete amphitheatre of Park Hill Flats to Park Square for Walk F.

Attercliffe

Approximate distance: 2 to 3½ miles
Start: From Park Square

Firth's Norfolk Works, Spear and Jackson's Aetna Works, most of Cammell's first Cyclops Works, Jessops, Dunford Hadfields, Jonas and Colver, Brown-Bayleys . . . The East End names that made Sheffield great gradually fade as memory becomes history. The factories crumble or are demolished and the areas around them are "regenerated" to adapt to modern industries that need less space and fewer people.

Yet Attercliffe today is much more than a tour round a forest of For Sale signs rusty with age. True, there are few houses to be seen – the terraces jammed within feet of

the factories that employed the people who lived in them are no more, the communities have been systematically dismantled and the roads now lead only to Memory Lane. But if you have even a hint of romantic nostalgia for Sheffield's dirtier and noisier industries, this is the walk for you – weaving up and down from the peace of the canal to the traffic racket of Attercliffe Road, the East End's two great arteries.

We start at Park Square (1) and, following the towpath sign, head briefly up the Parkway before turning left onto Blast Lane (named after the Old Park Blast Furnaces). To the left is the grand delapidation of the early nineteenth century canal basin – once the commercial heart of the city but last used for trade in 1970 and now given over to boat moorings under tarpaulin and pigeon roosts in warehouses. Not without reason is one of them called the Terminal Warehouse. Various schemes are underway to revitalise the area, but for the moment it is rather a case of deadlock in the dead locks. As well as the black and white warehouses, here's the Royal Victoria Hotel, splendid in its isolation on the vast viaduct that once included Victoria Station and still includes The Wicker.

Also on the left, through rose bay willow herb or Michaelmas daisies according to season, is the Sheaf Works, a fine classical 1820s structure from the days when chimneys smoked incessantly and washing never looked clean and factories pretended to be country houses. Before the railway bridge – an important milestone, or perhaps tombstone, in the canal's decline – turn left down a dank passage (2) where pigeons flutter and water drips from damp black stone into damp black

Walk F:

1
BLAST LANE
2
PARKWAY
3
CADMAN
ST.
SUSSEX ST.
LEVESON ST.
4
EFFINGHAM RD.
ATTERCLIFFE ROAD
5
WARREN ST.
WASHFORD BRIDGE
BACON LANE
6
LAWRENCE
ST.
ZION LANE
STANIFORTH RD.
7
9
8
VICARAGE RD.
WORKSOP
ROAD
10
LEEDS RD.

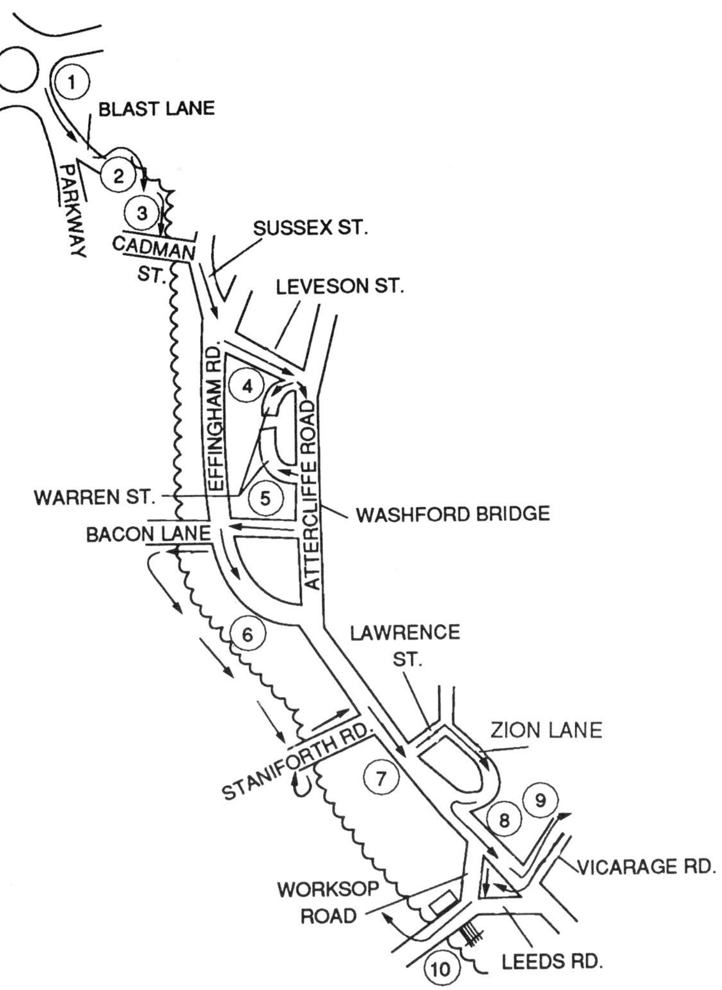

canal . . . the Sheffield and Tinsley Canal. Such stillness now, an ever-changing curve of brick factories and warehouses, corrugated iron, broken windows, tin cans, swooping dragonflies, moss, ferns, waterlilies, dead fish, rippled reflections, large unidentified lumps of rusting metal, mooring rings, low arched bridges (they had to squeeze the barges through), and walls built from grindstones. The only sounds are the distant hiss of machinery and the clatter of crossing trains. A self-contained world, insulated from the rest of Attercliffe, picturesque after decades of decay.

The canal threads a three-mile course through the East End, but is less weed-choked and silted than it once was, and no longer the colour of orange barley water now that the iron-oxided water of the Nunnery Colliery has ceased to be its main feed. It was cut through open fields in 1819, after a century of lobbying successfully opposed by the Dukes of Norfolk, who feared the easy

import of coal would threaten their own Sheffield pits. The canal had a very brief heyday – just nineteen years until the more economical Sheffield to Rotherham railway was built to supersede it. It still had its uses, though. Before the First World War, Thomas Firth and Son used it to bring 200,000 tons of Swedish iron to Sheffield – but, like the basin, it was last used in 1970 and, until a mid-1980s cleaning-up, was a refuse tip of bobbing tyres and floating fish and chip trays. A water rat would have thought twice about dying in here.

Our walk will eventually include the first mile or so of the canal but for the moment, having sampled the backwater atmosphere, leave it at the first round-arched bridge – at Cadman Street (3), one of the original fifteen bridges. (The whole canal walk has been admirably detailed in a separate East End History Trail published by Sheffield City Libraries.) Left up the cobbled path from the towpath, ignoring the far-from-picturesque pipeline disfiguring the bridge, and turn right into a strangely peaceful atmosphere of Victorian factories. In places, the walls seem to be suffering some virulent skin disease, their bricks covered by random rashes of different shades of red. Carry on along Sussex Street, under the bridge, past the one-time North Pole pub – before the canal came, a private house called Parkside Cottage. Cross onto Leveson Street, perhaps venturing up to Attercliffe Station for a real frontier outpost feel. Cross Norfolk Bridge (4) – not the railway bridge (the traditional start of Attercliffe), but the bridge over the River Don, with CH for Charles Howard (Duke of Norfolk) worked into its pitted ironwork. Over to the right of the bridge is Salmon

Pastures, where in 1850, apprenticeship agreements stated: "Masters should not compel the lad to eat salmon more than twice per week." Nature is now gradually returning here, though as yet there are neither salmon nor pastures.

At the traffic lights, bear right onto Warren Street, where the Norfolk Arms, like many East End pubs, spreads itself comfortably round a corner site to provide a reassuring landmark. With its brightly shining tiles and its frosted windows, it promised nights of happy oblivion. Such pubs are practically the only domestic-scale architecture left in Attercliffe. The houses that gave them a human context – and daily trade – have largely gone, so many are sadly boarded up. Large tracts of this area now have a melancholy air; deserted Victorian townships can be as desolate as deserted medieval villages. But bear with the next 400 yards or so, even though they are not over-pretty.

Turn down cobbled Warren Street to Spencer's Norfolk Bridge Works, a small 1868 factory building. On a miniature scale, it presents many of the typical features of Attercliffe's factories – a solid curving frontage, round-topped windows, a compact office (with double doors and a brass plaque . . . even the humblest factory ran to a brass plaque), and a confident ornamental archway with a little house for the gatekeeper, a rack for clock cards (now in some cases a nostalgic memento) and a pinned-up copy of the Factories Act. The street is blocked off, so back to Attercliffe Road and right, past Carter and Sons brick frontage – like a vast dovecote – to its other end, where Salmon Pastures School (5) is a fine 1908 memorial to the Victorian-cum-Edwardian vision of education as aspiration. Tall, as solid as the teaching of the Three Rs going on inside, and as unpredictably planned, with its towers and bays, as most of its pupils' futures, it had big windows to let in the light of learning and is now, with its buff stone, cleaner than it has been for eighty years.

After Washford Bridge, turn right along the path that follows the River Don, right at the top and across Effingham Road. Turn left along the front of the 1850 Baltic Works (6) – with four generations of window styles – as far as the War Memorial set in the wall. It commemorates the twenty-nine victims of the only Zeppelin raid on Sheffield – in 1916. Retrace steps to the end of the works, where metal strengtheners cover the wall like assorted sticking plasters, pause at the bridge for the canal views both ways (Park Hill looming towards town) and down the steps on the left. The blind bricked-up windows of the Spartan Works and the tufts of fern sprouting from every rusted hole add a melancholy air that is dispelled as soon as we return to street level at the Staniforth Road bridge (the next bridge on).

Turn right at the top and, past the white Art Deco doorway of Burtons building, head right into Attercliffe Road. The atmosphere suddenly perks up at the shopping centre, with its prosperous-looking banks full of overweeningly grand architecture. As befits temples to Mammon, they are a riot of scrolls, coats of arms and cherubs, the instant heraldry of Profit. Banners (7) (Bargains Are Our Business) makes a fine white flagship for the shopping centre, with its 1933 urns and canopies.

Now let out to small retailers, it doesn't perhaps have the thrill of a big department store, but it's still thriving. Just along, Beeley's Sandwich Corner is a real, pull-down-blind corner shop (Henderson's Relish generally in the window) and there's Betty's Hair Salon, with its black shiny fascia and its oh-so-elegant Woman's Realm lettering and its mauve net curtains.

The cobbled streets are out in force here . . . Baltic Lane and, across the road, Zion Lane leading off Lawrence Street. Go down the lane round from the Zion Sabbath School, the only relic of the now demolished Hammer Horror Zion Chapel, and, at the end, right and sharp left through the gates into Attercliffe Cemetery (8) on the site of the blitzed Christ Church, a windswept desolate place where the gravestones stand blackly to attention around the walls. Under the row of trees that bisects the churchyard, the gravestone of John Fareham Sephton (three graves from the right) suggests Victorian stonemasons did not always scrupulously learn their Salmon Pastures lessons:

"Remember as thou passert by,
As thou art now, so wonce was I."

Return to the gate and turn left to glance up Vicarage Road, where the 1920 Adelphi Cinema (9) – Attercliffe's

grandest – piles up its ornamental arches in the best Late Hindu style of cinema architecture and cross the road, where the manorial Free Library and Baths are now isolated in a wasteland of emptiness. Back towards town and turn left down Worksop Road past the 1772 Britannia Pub's more recent frontage aligning it with the road. Carry on as far as the Canal Aqueduct (10) – a Grade II listed structure. From below, this squat, splayed-out, curving black 1819 landmark, with its road and pedestrian tunnels dipping underneath, looks like an ordinary bridge (best seen from the far side). But the water dripping on the moss and pigeon droppings gives the game away. Go up the steps on the right and you enter a world away from urban Attercliffe. The canal, here again as if by magic, is now complete with chirping birds and ducks and an even more tranquil air. If this were in Camden, people would come from miles around to see it at weekends. From here walk back along the canal with a choice of leaving at Staniforth Road, Bacon Lane, Lumley Street, leading into Bernard Road, or Cadman Street. Or go right back to Park Square.

West Bar and Parkwood Springs

Approximate distance: 2 miles
Start: From Church Street

Our hands get ever grimier the farther we go on this walk, from the professional heart of the city to the manufacturing lungs. But first, for a glimpse of what might have been, to Sheffield Cathedral (1), a building easily taken for granted. It wouldn't have been if the planners had had their way. After the Second War, the Corporation – Alderman Sterland and Alderman Ballard and Alderman Keeble Hawson and Alderman Mrs. Tebbutt – had a dazzling vision of a Socialist New Jerusalem. Full of "noble buildings", it was "conceived on bold lines and in the high spirit of social service and dedication of self to a common cause". Castle Square and the Inner Ring Roads, the Polytechnic and Pond Street Bus Station all grew from this Utopian dream, which was too full of radical confidence to worry about such niceties as conservation. Much was to be swept away, but the Cathedral, inconveniently outside the main scheme, would be rebuilt on unimaginably grand lines, with two spires and a realigned nave bigger than any aircraft hangar. Like much of the plan, the Cathedral never left the drawing board, but it makes the 1966 extensions seem tactfully modest.

From the Cathedral entrance, turn left and left again into East Parade, a picture postcard procession of Georgian and Victorian Gothic, and pass reverently the augustly stooping statue of James Montgomery (1771-1854), editor of the Sheffield Iris newspaper. Ahead, across Campo Lane, is St Peter's Close (2). The next hundred yards includes three of the handful of surviving

Walk G:

10
WALLACE RD.
BARDWELL
ROAD
RUTLAND ROAD
9
8
BALL ST.
7
6
COTTON ST.
CORNISH
STREET
GREEN LANE
BOWER SPRING
5
WEST BAR
4
WEST BAR GN.
2
3
EAST
PARADE
1
CHURCH ST.

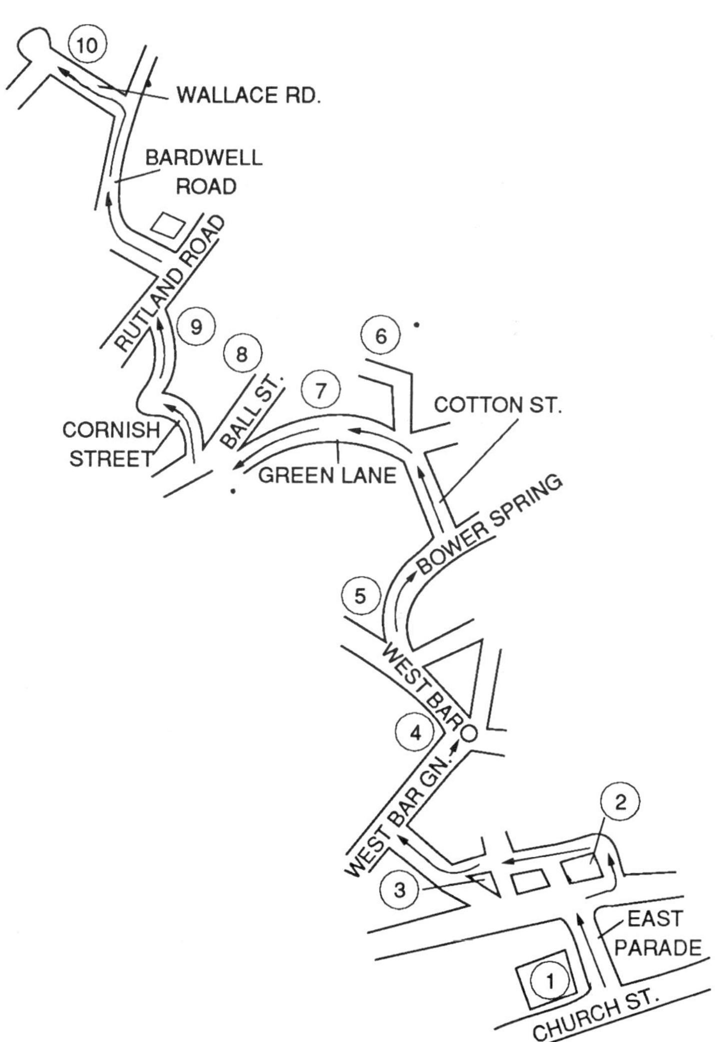

city centre gas lamps (all blue-painted and nicely ornate). Two are in the Close itself, full of bends and bumps and all manner of impediments to modern traffic. At the end, turn right into North Church Street, past the splendidly 1940s "My Own Toilet Preparations" sign and left into the legal world of Wheats Lane, with its offices as black as a lawyer's gown. We emerge in Paradise Square (3), a grand place to screw a brass plaque to your own respectability. A slope of winter-slippy car-cluttered cobbles, it was once a market place where John Wesley celebratedly preached. The plaque to this 1779 crowd-puller, over on the top side, was unveiled by J. Arthur Rank, no less, in 1951. Sheffield-born sculptor Sir Francis Chantrey had a studio here, but the most intriguing bit of local history is the plaque at the bottom corner – to David Daniel Davis (1778-1841), who translated a respected Treatise on Insanity and, as if that weren't enough, "assisted at the birth of Queen Victoria".

Cross the square and continue down Silver Street, with the Three Tuns pub surging forward like a proudly prowed sailing ship, go right into West Bar Green and pause at the South Yorkshire Fire Services Museum. It's worth a visit, if only to admire the solid scarlet and brass Dennis Big Four, every Dinky Toy collector's dream of a fire engine, and to learn that brass firemen's helmets gave way to leather ones in the mid 1930s when electric light became standard and firemen were anxious not to electrocute themselves by catching cables.

To the left, West Bar was once the Shaftesbury Avenue of the Sheffield working man – a warren of music halls. The 1,500-seat Casino (complete with its own waxworks), the London Apprentice, the Bijou . . . in their Victorian heyday, Sheffield boasted more music halls than any other city outside London. Most were built in the 1850s and 1860s onto the backs of public houses and were

rough and ready places with a saloon bar atmosphere. In the shop next to the fire museum are the remains of the Britannia (4), one of Britain's last half-dozen surviving halls. Dan Leno clattered through his clog dance here, Louis Metzger (owner and pork butcher) made the most of Lucy his musical pig and 1,000 people regularly applauded. The Brit closed in the 1890s, as keener licensing laws tightened up the fire regulations and the growth of Variety in the bigger theatres brought star turns with whom the smaller halls couldn't compete. Today, behind locked doors and up creaking stairs, the Brit's relics, most visibly the proscenium arch, are in a sad state of decay.

Across the road, on the corner of Steelhouse Lane and Corporation Street, the paint-flaking remains of the smaller Gaiety Music Hall are now hidden behind the modern interior walls of part of Ellis, Son and Paramore's surgical appliance factory. Specialists in the bespoke truss, E S and P are a fine old Sheffield firm who, in their labryinth of workshops, have been helping Nature along with their Single Spring Truss and their Double Spring Truss since 1780. They enjoyed vast sales during the heyday of Britain's battleships, when all shells had to be lifted by hand.

Glance up Lambert Street at the solid 1765 Times-style lettering of John Watts and Son ("Stampers, Piercers and Metal Workers," it proclaims, as though words are at no premium. "Safety Razors, Scissors, Skates"). Cross West Bar to Bower Spring for the remains of two 1830 conical brick cementation furnaces (5) – blister steel predecessors of the crucible steel method.

Turn into cobbled Cotton Street, so narrow its double yellow lines almost meet in the middle, and enter the maze of light engineering businesses around Kelham Island Industrial Museum (6). Left into Alma Street and pause at the Wire Workers Union offices (until the mid

1980s more resoundingly named the Amalgamated Society of Wire Drawers and Kindred Workers). Here is an optional detour into Kelham Island, where most of the exhibits make a hell of a row and earn their keep as they would have done in their working days – the days when the Atlas and Cyclops steelworks mythology hid appalling conditions, as we shall see round the next corner.

Kelham Island – genuinely an island between the Don and a picturesquely weed-choked, slime-silted mill race – has produced its own Museum Round Trail, which gives admirable historical detail on the next few streets. Glance at the Globe Steelworks, once the Sheffield Workhouse, with its peeling green globe (not peeling over Great Britain, you'll note) and carry on past the Fat Cat pub into Green Lane. On the left is the former Ebenezer Wesleyan Chapel of 1823, a splendid Gothic fantasy that could pass as a folly in the grounds of a Shropshire country house. Victorian churchmen guard its Ebenezer Place door, and the initials of a whole pew-full of worthies (EBF and SMJ and TMN and AAJ) punctuate its stonework.

Green Lane boasted, or perhaps kept very quiet about, some of Sheffield's worst housing conditions. In 1857 the courts and yards bounded by the lane, Acorn Street, Shalesmoor and Dun Street were packed with 473 people in a hundred households, plus a foundry, a brewery and two pubs. Just along is the grand triumphal gateway of the Green Lane Works (7), where proprietor Henry E. Hoole (Mayor in 1860) had his name carved on the artist's palette and Vulcan's anvil in the tableaux on either side. Left into Ball Street to glimpse, among

tangled weeds and pigeon droppings, the great 1828 river frontage of James Dixon's Cornish Place factory (8), a sheer cliff face of 114 windows. Built when gracious salmon swam in the gracious River Don, it was Sheffield's

first large-scale factory (four acres) and was celebrated worldwide for its silver, silver plate and Britannia metal. Engravings from 1880 show pluming James Dixon smoke and strutting James Dixon horses and an overall atmosphere of James Dixon urgency. Today, where brass plaques once gleamed resplendent, the factory's tenants are happy just to chalk their names on the entrance arch.

Back for a glimpse of the soberly stylish Globe Works, looking out for the plethora of plaster signs, and down Cornish Street, with its overwhelming atmosphere of dark drudgery. Go to the very end and turn into the riverside

Waterloo Walk (9) for the fine river frontages on the right, cross Rutland Road, left into Neepsend Lane, and up Bardwell Road under the railway arch to Parkwood Springs (10).

Here is one of Sheffield's strangest, most desolate landscapes. Once it was a "forgotten village" of 350 houses and a 1,000-strong hill-tribe community. Known as the Lost Horizon, it was finally pulled down in 1975

and its residents dispersed over Sheffield. But its name, suggesting Spa resorts and garden suburbs, remains. The steep bald outcrop of scrubland, a prime site for an Iron Age hill fort if only the Iron Age folk had thought of it, offers a spectacular 600 feet panorama of the city, from Andover Street, across the concrete snake of Kelvin, past Crookes and Hillsborough out to Oughtibridge. Not pretty, but very Sheffield. Parkwood Springs, cut off from the rest of Sheffield on the other side of the tracks (literally) developed a strong identity with its half-dozen corner shops and beer-offs and its reputation for bracing Blackpool air. It had no doctor, no Post Office and, until the 1970s, no bus service (and then just three times a day on Tuesdays and Fridays). Now there are only dumped sofas and motor-cycle scramblers re-creating the TT races. But the cobbles and the cellar grates are a peculiarly melancholy reminder of a place where people once lived. People like Eb Sales with his flower in his button hole, Old Man Danks in his moleskins, Brum George the gamekeeper . . . recent mythology to add to the recent archaeology of the Springs. We drop down the path at the far end of Wallace Road, cross the railway bridge, past Neepsend Gasworks, where the magpies clatter (Sheffield has more than any other city) and, at the end of Hoyland Road, cross Hillfoot Bridge and climb Wood Street for an 81/2/3/4 bus back to the city centre from Infirmary Road. On the way, just past the Globe Works, glimpse on the right Bradleys boarded-up shop – "Boots, Shoes and Clogs". Doubtless by appointment to Parkwood Springs. Or, instead of the bus, turn left into Infirmary Road and Walk H.

Upperthorpe, Walkley and Crookesmoor

Approximate distance: 2 miles
Start: Buses Nos 81/2/3/4 from city centre to old Royal Infirmary

The people of Walkley – if old photographs are to be believed – were always, and appropriately, walking. Walking on Whit Walks, walking on Scout and Girl Guide processions, walking – **strenuously** walking – up and down the hills on which their urban village is so firmly screwed down. Walking rather than waiting for the trams that would, eventually, lurch over the switchback hills from Sheffield.

So our walk is, as a sort to tribute, the most arduously uphill of the series. We start in Infirmary Road outside the Royal Infirmary (1) – Sheffield's first hospital, opened in 1797. The original building, with its sedate pillared frontage flanked by gracious bays, has its purpose spelt out over the doorway in church-fearing gold letters: "I was sick and ye visited me." And stands the clock at half past six, permanently. Head towards Kelvin Flats, dominating the area on such a callously inhuman scale, and left up Albert Terrace Road, past the grandly Parisian nurses' home. At the junction, turn right into Upperthorpe Road and back into the 1940s.

We shall find time more dramatically suspended in Walkley, but for the moment here is time suspended in miniature – Upperthorpe shopping centre (2) with Ansons Hairdressing Saloon and the Upperthorpe Hotel ("A warm welcome from your hosts Pat/Jack") and a whole cluster of wall adverts for Beaufoys Famous Tent Wines (2/- per quart) and Fields Pecto (Cures Coughs and Colds – 1/3 and 2/6 per bottle). And a truly local post

office, with handwritten postcards advertising a Mobile Hairdresser (phone Deborah), Twin Tub Washing Machines, a Bontempi Electronic Organ, and "Beautiful jade green fur jacket – ideal gift". This is as important a strand of the fabric of everyday Sheffield corner shop life as the grand statues on Upperthorpe Library – a pity the communities such corner shops served have so often been dispersed.

Follow Upperthorpe Road past the library and up into Daniel Hill, taking the raised pavement path, and climb the cobbles of Daniel Hill Walk (3), a gennel of punishing steepness. Past Upperthorpe First and Middle Schools, centres of high altitude education, and left at the top into Daniel Hill Street. The terraces snake up and down – uniquely Sheffield terraces where no householder has the same number of front steps as his neighbour. Past Blake

Walk H:

ALBERT
TERRACE
ROAD
INFIRMARY ROAD
BIRKENDALE VIEW
SOUTH
ROAD
HOWARD
ROAD
DANIEL HILL ST.
BIRKENDALE RD.
DANIEL
HILL
UPPERTHORPE RD
BIRKENDALE
BARBER RD.
CROOKES VALLEY
ROAD
COMMONSIDE
MUSHROOM
LANE
WESTERN BANK
1
2
3
4
5
6
7
8
9
10

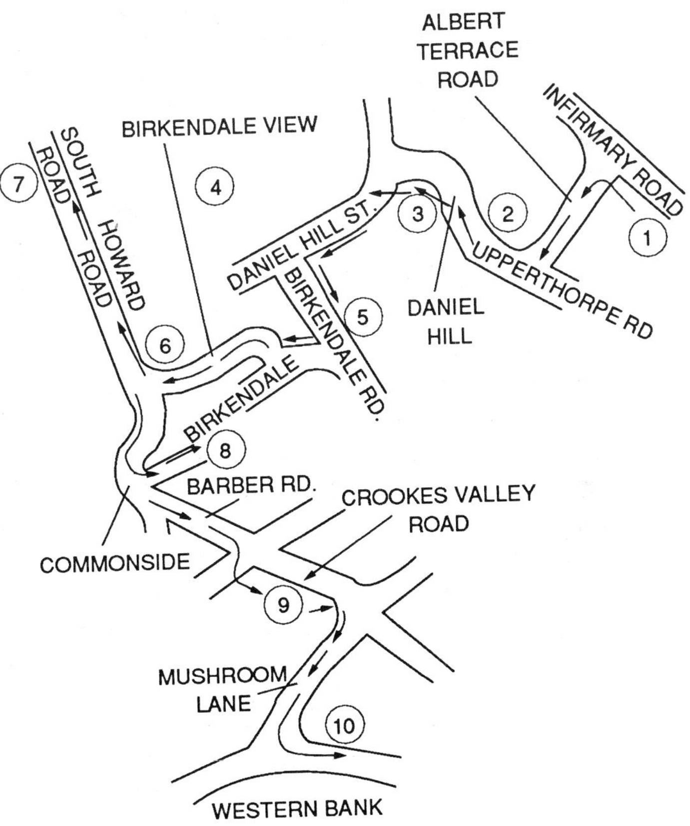

Street, with Ruskin Park (4) on the right (Ruskin's first museum was some distance away, between Bole Hill Road and Bell Hagg Road on Walkley Bank). Left along the path skirting a wooden fence and left again at the end when you are just expecting someone's backyard, and suddenly the birds are chirping and we are in Birkendale (5), a Victorian suburb of Bohemia.

It gets even better as we turn left down Birkendale

Road, right onto Birkendale pure and simple, and right again, round and up Birkendale View. This you wouldn't expect behind Kelvin – dark drives with towering laurel and holly bushes shielding grandly castellated stone villas. In this total seclusion from the rest of Walkley – and only the odd glimpse over the city centre to remind you where you are – trees ramble wildly and autumn pears fall on mattresses of dead leaves to rot unattended. Here is Holyrood House and a host of typically thin detached Walkley homes, their windows crammed with heraldic stained glass shields, and their no-nonsense stone gateposts bearing Cave Canem notices to advise us

that the owners keep a Latin dog of which we should beware, lest it snap at our genitives. At the top, turn right through the wrought-iron gate (6) and a great whoosh of traffic brings us back to Howard Road and the late twentieth century.

But not for long. To the right, Howard Road and South Road offer ceaseless fascination until they come to an abrupt full stop at Walkley Library (7), placed fair and square on its bracing corner. "Andrew Carnegie presented this library, 1905" announces the vestibule plaque. And here is Carnegie himself, gazing with manic philanthropy at the pinned up adverts for circus workshops and SWAPO benefit concerts. This is the new Walkley, following Broomhill along the path of radical chic – but the old Walkley is all around us on either side of the challengingly narrow and gloriously 1964 South Road (only just wide enough for two buses). Its little shops sell obscure things in small quantities with, at random, the Noted Bacon Shop, the Elégance Fashion Shop, the wholefoods shop, the wool shop for classic double knits, the sweet shop with its plastic spearmint dispensers, drapers selling men's string briefs, herbalists selling

Potter's Sugar Cane Molasses, and a second-hand bookshop to put much of it in perspective with The Culture of the Abdomen.

The Victorian streets running off this "main" road, with its Hovis signs, were unchanged for a century until the late 1980s, when many were blocked off. But though Walkley thrived under Victoria, its history goes back to Saxon times. Cutlery, inevitably, was the mainstay, with its Tudor population of 200 working mostly as grinders and cutlers at wheels in the Rivelin Valley.

Explore it at leisure and return to the wrought-iron gate for the road back to town. The view over Sheffield is predictably spectacular and, as Commonside sweeps broadly round, the sense of space is a real surprise. Down Upperthorpe (8) are fine Victorian houses, and Steel Bank Villas on the right of Commonside – up a set of steps between the shop fronts – have their own novel high-level terrace. A little further, one of the city's most elegant public toilets is embedded under an archway in the wall (the standard work on Sheffield's public conveniences has yet to be written). Follow Barber Road left towards the city centre. An unnamed street to the left opens into an unexpectedly bijoutified mews, and The Nook offers Sheffield's cutest address.

Past Crookesmoor Road, turn right down and through Crookes Valley Park (9), around a dam built in 1758, and at the end cross Crookes Valley Road to survey The Rec – whose access road, Mushroom Lane, is forever preserved as Sheffield's image to the outside world in Bill Brandt's celebrated 1930s photograph of a street lamp glowing under a foggy terrace of chimneys. Recross the road and turn right along the continuation of Mushroom Lane, with its pleasantly rural feel, and carry on round to Western Bank, where Weston Park (10) is famed for its bandstand, its tropical greenhouse, its 1859 column (by Godfrey Sykes – in turn famed for South Kensington Museum) and its 1854 statue – once in the Market Place – of "Corn Law Rhymer" Ebenezer Elliott ("What is a communist?" he ponders as he gazes not quite towards the Town Hall. "One who has yearnings/ For equal sharing of unequal earnings").

And of course, there is the Museum – don't miss the 1890 Japanese Sumo Wrestlers, large as life and twice as vicious, but with bits of offcut front room curtain knotted modestly round their waists. They have been a source of endless fascination for generations of Sheffield schoolboys among the Owls as Predators tableaux, and the Egyptian mummies without their wisdom teeth, and the Roberts and Belk fish forks.

Next door is the Mappin Art Gallery, built in 1887 as a bequest by industrialist John Newton Mappin ("Stout form and somewhat brusque manners", noted one newspaper). The gallery was once graced, to revive a small-type footnote of Sheffield art history, by a plaster copy of the Town Hall's statue of Vulcan. It had pride of place until it was destroyed by a 1940 bomb targetted by Nazis with a perverse hatred of the sort of Victorian art with which the gallery was still stocked. The story goes that, while sifting through the wreckage, an attendant discovered Vulcan's vital organ, quite intact. With a nice line in enterprise, he took it home to use as a doorknocker, and subsequent efforts to retrieve it as council property came to nothing. They had not thought of that, of course, at the early events held here – the British Medical Association civic reception and garden party, or the British Empire Shakespeare Society Annual Conversazione (Carriages at 10.15). Before you step inside the Mappin, be warned that the original rules and regulations specified sternly: "Visitors must be cleanly in person and dress, and shall not bring wet umbrellas or other objectionable objects into the gallery." From here, it is a pleasant walk or a quick 52 bus ride down the hill into town for a new pair of shoes. Or a 52 **up** the hill to start Walk A again.